STEP-BY-STEP
Sentences

LINWORTH LEARNING

From the Minds of Teachers

Linworth Publishing, Inc.
Worthington, Ohio

Cataloging-in-Publication Data

Editor: Claire Morris

Design and Production: Good Neighbor Press, Inc.

Published by Linworth Publishing, Inc.
480 East Wilson Bridge Road, Suite L
Worthington, Ohio 43085

ISBN: 1-58683-146-1

5 4 3

Table of Contents

Introduction

Step-by-Step Sentences is designed to motivate and engage students who may have difficulty with language. Skills are addressed in a variety of fun and interesting formats to accommodate individual learning styles. Each skill is introduced according to a developmental progression and at low readability levels to promote success and understanding. Activity sheets have clear and simple instructions, examples,and exercises which may include word manipulation, understanding pictorial cues, and problem-solving. Assessment activities follow the format of standardized tests and require students to eliminate incorrect options, choose the correct answer, and fill in the appropriate circle. The material in this book correlates with the national curriculum standards for Grades 1–2 and covers the following skills: identifying complete and incomplete sentences, identifying declarative and interrogative sentences, recognizing and using correct word order, and finding the subject (who or what?) and predicate (does what?). An answer key is provided at the back of the book.

Sentence or Not?

Directions:

Look at the pairs of pictures.

Circle the picture that shows a complete thought.

Make an X over the picture that shows an incomplete thought.

1. The girl.  The girl bakes cookies.

2. The boy rides his bike.  The bike.

3. The man cuts grass.  The man.

4. The baby.  The baby takes a nap.

5. The girl throws the ball.  The ball.

Sentence Puzzles

Directions:

Read each group of words.

If the words make a sentence, color the puzzle pieces yellow.

If the words do not make a sentence, color the puzzle pieces blue.

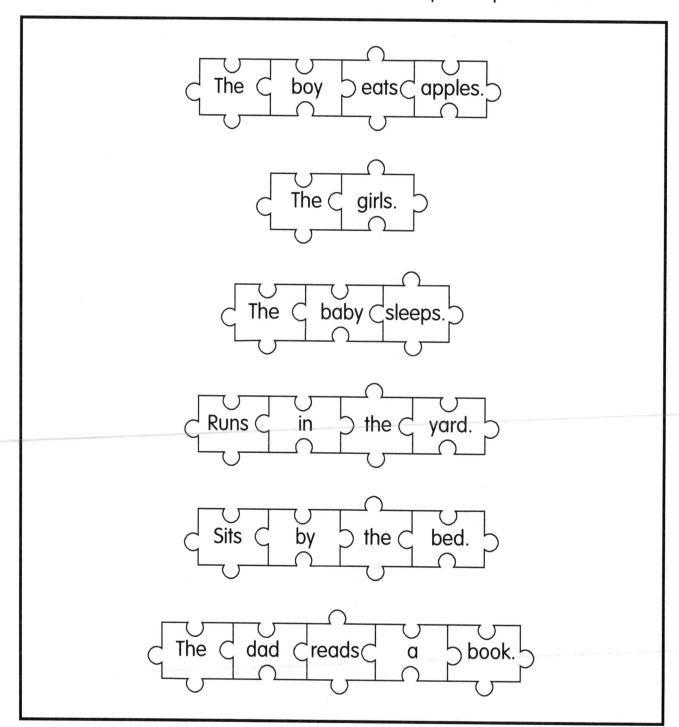

The | boy | eats | apples.

The | girls.

The | baby | sleeps.

Runs | in | the | yard.

Sits | by | the | bed.

The | dad | reads | a | book.

Name_____ Date_____

# Is It a Sentence?

Directions:
Read each group of words.
If the words make a sentence, draw a picture for the sentence in the box.
If the words do not make a sentence, make and X in the box.

1. The man cooks lunch.	2. The cow.
3. Plays a game.	4. The cat climbs a tree.
5. The duck swims in the pond.	6. The frog jumps on a log.

Sorting Sentences

Directions:
Read each group of words.
Cut out each group of words, and glue it in the correct box.

Sentence

Not a Sentence

The bird sings.

The dog.

Talks to me.

The baby sleeps.

He takes the bus.

Rides his bike.

Asking Sentences

Directions:

Read each group of words.

If the group of words is an asking sentence, color the bubble yellow.

If the group of words is not an asking sentence, color the bubble blue.

1. What are?

2. What are you doing?

3. Can?

4. Will she have a party?

5. Who is?

6. Does she like cake?

More Asking Sentences

Directions:
Read the invitation below.
Then read each group of words.
If the group of words makes an asking sentence, answer the question.
If the group of words is not an asking sentence, circle the group of words.

Ryan will have a party!
You will spend the night at my house.
You need to bring a pillow.
We will eat pizza!
We will play games!
We will stay up all night!
Please come to my party!

1. Who will have a party?   Ryan

2. Where will?

3. What does?

4. What will they play?

5. What will they eat?

Sorting Asking Sentences

Directions:

Read each group of words.

Cut out each group of words, and glue it in the correct box.

Asking Sentence

Not a Sentence

Who is he?	Who will go to?
Will you sing a song?	Can I read to you?
Run with you?	Where do?

Making Complete Sentences

Directions:

Look at each picture.

Read the words next to it.

Make the group of words a sentence by drawing a line to its missing part.

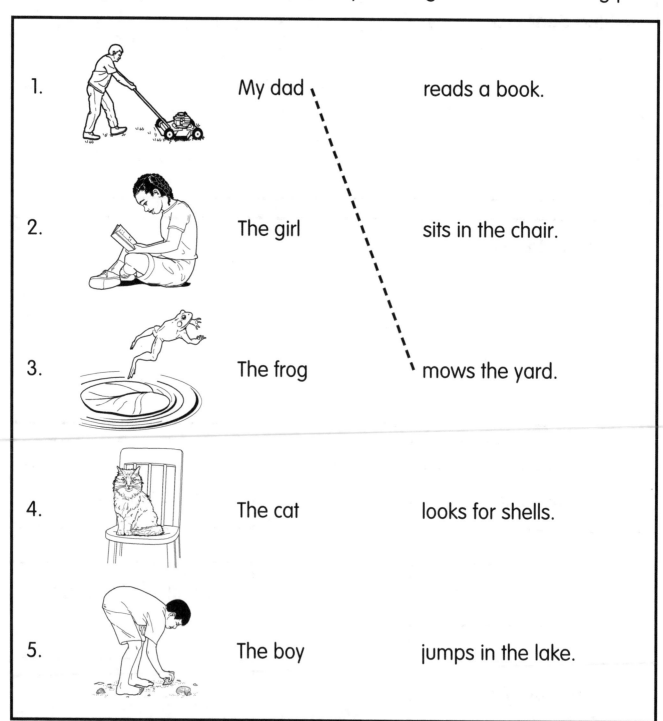

1.   My dad   reads a book.

2.   The girl   sits in the chair.

3.   The frog   mows the yard.

4.   The cat   looks for shells.

5.   The boy   jumps in the lake.

Name_____ Date_____

Making Complete Sentences

Directions:
Look at each picture.
Read the words next to it.
Make the group of words a sentence by drawing a line to its missing part.

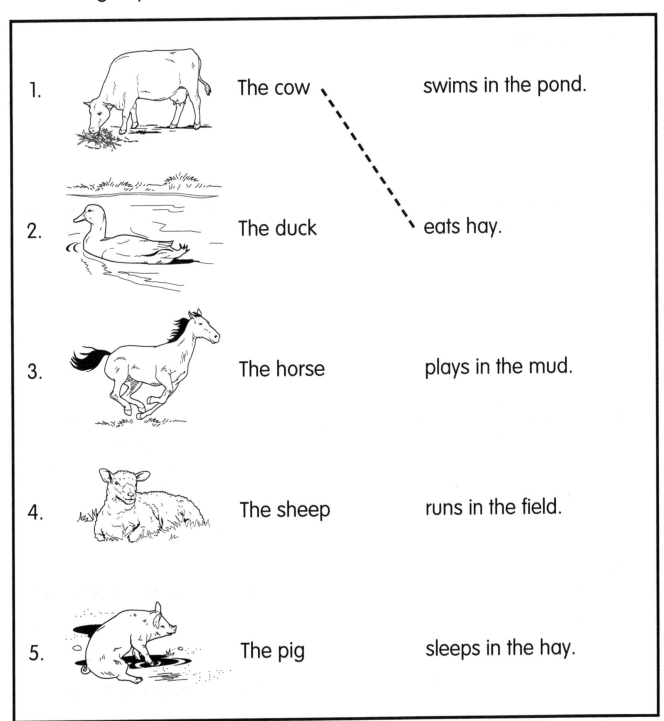

1.	The cow		swims in the pond.
2.	The duck		eats hay.
3.	The horse		plays in the mud.
4.	The sheep		runs in the field.
5.	The pig		sleeps in the hay.

Asking or Telling Sentences

Directions:
Read each group of words.
Cut out each group of words.
Glue it in the correct box to make a sentence.

```
┌─────────────────────────────────────────────┐
│ Asking Sentence                              │
│                                              │
│                                              │
│                                              │
│                                              │
│                                              │
└─────────────────────────────────────────────┘
```

```
┌─────────────────────────────────────────────┐
│ Telling Sentence                             │
│                                              │
│                                              │
│                                              │
│                                              │
│                                              │
└─────────────────────────────────────────────┘
```

Will you ride your bike?

We ride bikes.

She plays soccer.

Do you like to play soccer?

Can you climb a tree?

The boy likes to climb trees.

Ordering Words in Sentences

Directions:

Read each group of words.

Cut out each group of words, and glue them in the correct order.

1.

2.

3.

4.

party?	to	going	Who	is	the
talks	She	on	phone.		the
pictures.	draw	We	to	like
eat	for	he	What	lunch?	does

Asking or Telling Sentences

Directions:

Read each group of words.

Decide whether it is an asking or a telling sentence.

Draw a line to the **A** if it is an asking sentence.

Draw a line to the **T** if it is a telling sentence.

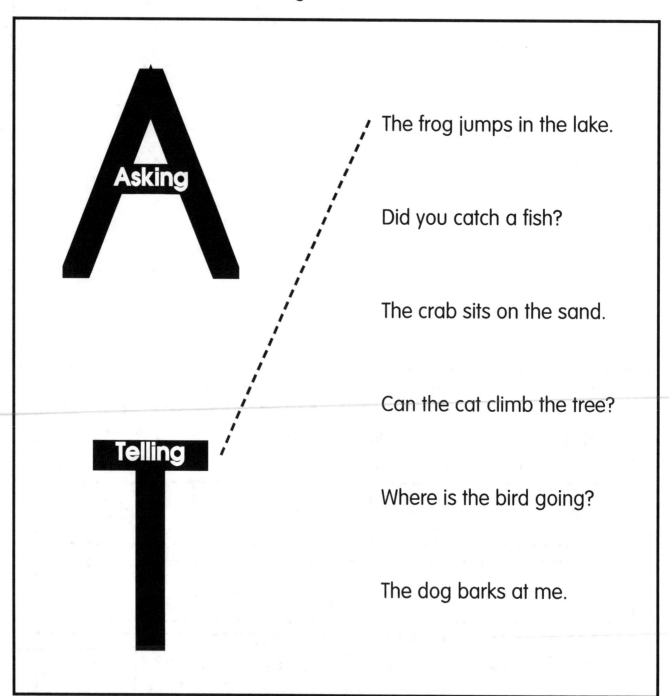

A Asking

T Telling

The frog jumps in the lake.

Did you catch a fish?

The crab sits on the sand.

Can the cat climb the tree?

Where is the bird going?

The dog barks at me.

Identifying Sentences

Directions:

Read each group of words.

If the group of words is a telling sentence, write **T** on the blank line.

If the group of words is an asking sentence, write **A** on the blank line.

If the group of words is not a sentence, write **N** on the blank line.

1. __A__   What color is your hair?

2. _____   My eyes are blue.

3. _____   See very far.

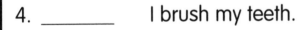

4. _____   I brush my teeth.

5. _____   Wash hands.

6. _____   Do you smell cookies?

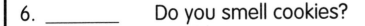

Writing Sentences

Directions:

Read each group of words.

Use the words to make an asking and a telling sentence.

Write the sentences on the lines.

---

1. help   will   you   me

Asking: <u>Will you help me?</u>

Telling: <u>You will help me.</u>

---

2. will   to   me   you   read

Asking: _____

Telling: _____

---

3. cake   do   like   you

Asking: _____

Telling: _____

---

4. a   can   ride   bike   you

Asking: _____

Telling: _____

---

5. you   my   are   friend

Asking: _____

Telling: _____

Reflect and Review

Directions:

Read each group of words.

If the group of words is not a sentence, circle the words.

If the group of words is an asking sentence, underline the sentence.

If the group of words is a telling sentence, underline the sentence two times.

1. <u>The girl finds a shell.</u>

2. Will you swim in the ocean?

3. The boys.

4. I like to go to the beach.

5. In the sand.

Who or What Part

Directions:
Read each sentence.
Circle the **who** or **what** part of the sentence.

1. (The boy) climbs a tree.

2. The dog bites a bone.

3. The cat sleeps on a chair.

4. The bird sings a song.

5. The dad cooks lunch.

6. The mom makes the bed.

Does What Part

Directions:

Read each sentence.

Circle the **does what** part of the sentence.

1. The frog (hops on a lily pad)

2. The fish swims in the lake.

3. The bear catches a fish.

4. The bird sits on a branch.

5. The goat eats grass.

6. The sheep drinks water.

Parts of a Sentence

Directions:

Read each sentence.

Draw a picture showing the **who** or **what** and the **does what** parts.

1. The boy kicks the ball.	2. The girl reads a book.
3. The pig sleeps in the mud.	4. The cat plays with yarn.
5. The duck swims in the lake.	6. The crab sits on the sand.

Identifying Parts of a Sentence

Directions:
Read each sentence.
Circle the **who** or **what** part.
Underline the **does what** part.

1. (The man) drives his car.

2. The girl kicks the ball.

3. The boy swings the bat.

4. The mom sings a song.

5. The dad reads a book.

6. The dog barks at the cat.

Identifying Parts of a Sentence

Directions:
Look at each picture.
Read the sentence beside it.
Answer the questions.

---

1. The girl opens the gift.

   Who or what? _____ the girl _____

   Does what? _____

---

2. The frog eats a fly.

   Who or what? _____

   Does what? _____

---

3. The sun shines.

   Who or what? _____

   Does what? _____

---

4. The cat sleeps on my lap.

   Who or what? _____

   Does what? _____

Making Complete Sentences

Directions:
Look at each picture.
Read the words next to it.
Make the group of words a sentence by drawing a line to its missing part.

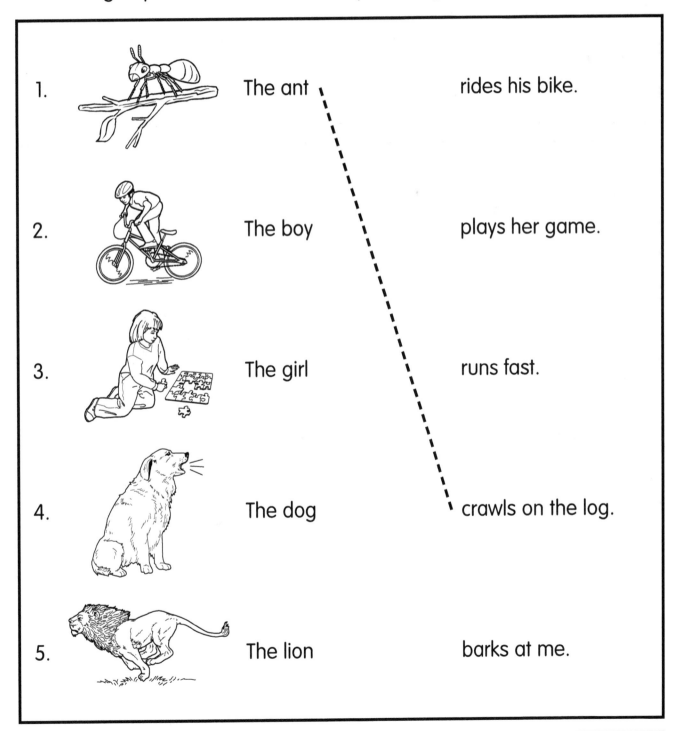

1. The ant — rides his bike.

2. The boy — plays her game.

3. The girl — runs fast.

4. The dog — crawls on the log.

5. The lion — barks at me.

Writing Complete Sentences

Directions:

Look at the picture.

Read each **who** or **what** part beside it.

Choose the correct **does what** part from the choices below.

Write the word on the line.

Does What?				
bite	talks	smells	sees	hear

1. The eye _____ sees _____.

2. The nose _____.

3. The ears _____.

4. The mouth _____.

5. The teeth _____.

Sentence Puzzles

Directions:

Read each puzzle piece.

Cut them out, and find the parts that go together.

Glue the parts together on a new page to make five sentences.

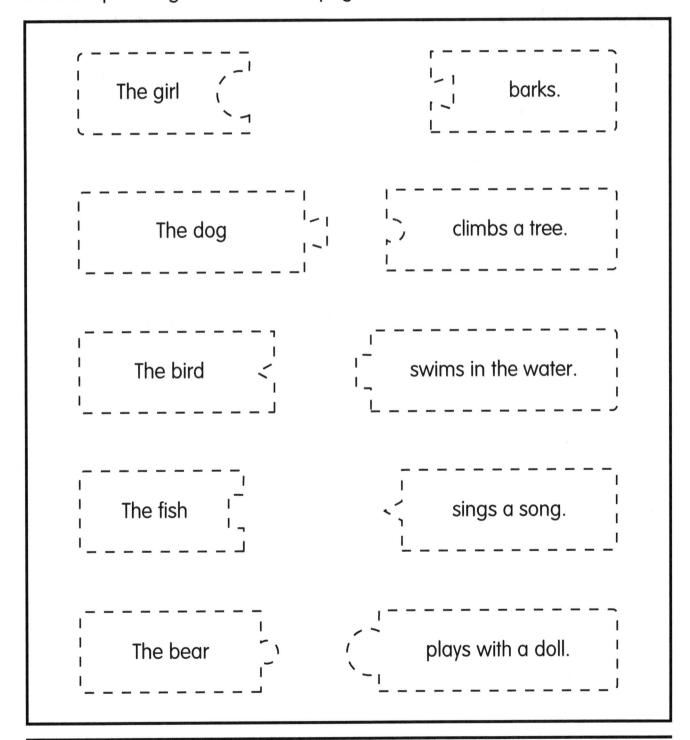

The girl

barks.

The dog

climbs a tree.

The bird

swims in the water.

The fish

sings a song.

The bear

plays with a doll.

Making Complete Sentences

Directions:

Read each group of words.

Draw a line from the **who** or **what** part to the correct **does what** part.

Who or What?	Does What?
1. The sun	falls from the tree.
2. The apple	crawls on a log.
3. The ant	lives in a cave.
4. The baby	shines in the sky.
5. The cake	sleeps in a bed.
6. The bat	bakes in an oven.

Finding the Who or What Part

Directions:
Look at the picture.
Read each **does what** part.
Choose the correct **who** or **what** part from the choices below.
Write the words on the lines.

Who or What?				
The bird	The girl	The boy	The cat	The dog

1. _____The girl_____ jumps rope.

2. _____ kicks a ball.

3. _____ sleeps in the yard.

4. _____ runs fast.

5. _____ sings in the tree.

Who or What & Does What Parts

Directions:
Read each sentence.
Write each part of the sentence in the correct box.

1. The dog runs.

2. The fish swims.

3. The bird sings a song.

4. The frog hops.

5. The horse eats hay.

Who or What?	Does What?
1. _The dog_____	1. _____runs_____
2. _____	2. _____
3. _____	3. _____
4. _____	4. _____
5. _____	5. _____

Name_____ Date_____

Who or What & Does What Parts

Directions:
Read each sentence.
Color the **who** or **what** parts red.
Color the **does what** parts yellow.

red ⟶		yellow ⟶		
The	duck	looks	for	food.

The	cat	climbs	the	tree.

The	fox	hides	by	a	rock.

The	fish	swims	in	the	pond.

The	goat	eats	grass.

Ordering Words in Sentences

Directions:

Read each group of words.

Cut out the words, and glue each one in the correct order.

1.

2.

3.

4.

| boy | plays | The | ball. |

| The | rope. | jumps | girl |

| sleeps. | The | baby |

| barks. | The | dog |

Finding Parts of a Sentence

Directions:
Read each sentence.
Underline the **who** or **what** part.
Circle the **does what** part.

1. The sheep stands in a field.

2. The cow eats grass.

3. The hen lays eggs.

4. The dog barks at the cat.

5. The duck quacks.

6. The pig rolls in the mud.

Reflect and Review

Directions:

Read each group of words.

If the group of words is not a sentence, color it yellow.

If the group of words is a sentence, color the **who** or **what** parts blue and the **does what** parts red.

blue ⟶		red ⟶	
The	boy	eats	lunch.

The	girl	sings	songs.

The	big	cat.

The	man	reads	a	book.

The	baby.

The	dog	barks.

Assessment 1

Directions:
Read each group of words.
Fill in the circle in front of the complete sentence.

1. ○ Goes to the store.

   ○ My friend.

   ◉ My friend goes to the store.

2. ○ She rides a bike.

   ○ Rides a blue bike.

   ○ She.

3. ○ The school.

   ○ We ride to school on a bus.

   ○ Drives a bus.

4. ○ The man walks the dog.

   ○ The dog.

   ○ Walks the dog.

5. ○ The apple.

   ○ Falling from trees.

   ○ The apple falls from the tree.

Assessment 2

Directions:
Read each group of words.
Fill in the circle in front of the group of words that is not a
complete sentence.

1. ○ My friend plays at my house.

   ○ We play games.

   ◉ Eat all the food.

2. ○ We run a race.

   ○ Runs faster.

   ○ She wins the race.

3. ○ Going to fish.

   ○ We go fishing in the lake.

   ○ We like to fish.

4. ○ Hits the ball.

   ○ He hit the ball.

   ○ The boy swings the bat.

5. ○ Draws a picture.

   ○ The girl can draw.

   ○ I like to draw.

Assessment 3

Directions:
Read each group of words.
Fill in the circle in front of the asking sentence.

1. ○ Will?

   ◉ Will you help me?

   ○ Run for help?

2. ○ May I have one cookie?

   ○ Bake some?

   ○ What can?

3. ○ What are?

   ○ Going to eat?

   ○ What are you going to eat?

4. ○ To the store?

   ○ Will you ride your bike?

   ○ Riding your bike?

5. ○ Who is at the door?

   ○ The door?

   ○ Who is at?

Assessment 4

Directions:
Read each group of words.
Fill in the circle in front of the telling sentence.

---

1. ○ Can you climb that tree?

   ● I like to climb trees.

---

2. ○ The dog runs in the yard.

   ○ Do you see the dog?

---

3. ○ Where does the cat sleep?

   ○ The cat sleeps on my bed.

---

4. ○ I like red apples.

   ○ Do you like apples?

---

5. ○ My friend jumps rope.

   ○ Can you jump rope?

---

6. ○ What is your favorite color?

   ○ I like the color blue.

Assessment 5

Directions:
Look at each picture.
Read the words next to it.
Fill in the circle in front of the words that complete the sentence.

1. The girl _____.		○ sits in a chair.
		○ rides a bike.
		◉ jumps rope.

2. The frog _____.		○ eats flies.
		○ hops on a lily pad.
		○ swims in the pond.

3. The cat _____.		○ takes a nap.
		○ drinks milk.
		○ chases a mouse.

4. The bird _____.		○ sings a song.
		○ flies in the sky.
		○ eats a worm.

5. The pig _____.		○ runs in the field.
		○ eats hay.
		○ plays in the mud.

Assessment 6

Directions:

Read each sentence.

Fill in the circle under the **who** or **what** part.

1. <u>The fish</u> <u>swims in the lake.</u>

   ◉   ○

2. <u>My friend</u> <u>plays baseball.</u>

   ○   ○

3. <u>My dad</u> <u>drives a red car.</u>

   ○   ○

4. <u>The boy</u> <u>reads a book.</u>

   ○   ○

5. <u>My grandpa</u> <u>rides a bus.</u>

   ○   ○

6. <u>Her mom</u> <u>likes to watch the game.</u>

   ○   ○

Assessment 7

Directions:
Fill in the circle next to the **does what** part.

1. The baby looks for a toy.	○ The baby ◉ looks for a toy.
2. The boy plays baseball.	○ The boy ○ plays baseball.
3. The family eats lunch.	○ The family ○ eats lunch.
4. The teacher reads a book.	○ The teacher ○ reads a book.
5. The girl kicks a ball.	○ The girl ○ kicks a ball.
6. We go to the library.	○ We ○ go to the library.

Assessment 8

Directions:

Look at the picture.

Read each **who** or **what** part.

Fill in the circle next to the correct **does what** part.

1.	The baby	○ eats. ● sleeps. ○ plays.
2.	The dad	○ drives a bus. ○ plays a game. ○ cooks lunch.
3.	The cat	○ climbs a tree. ○ runs fast. ○ sleeps on the bed.
4.	The fish	○ looks at a worm. ○ eats a plant. ○ swims in the lake.
5.	The girl	○ listens to a song. ○ eats cake. ○ smells a flower.

Assessment 9

Directions:

Look at the picture.

Read each sentence.

Fill in the circle under the correct **who** or **what** part.

1. _____ sits on a bench.

    The grandma   The man   The girl

        ●   ○   ○

2. _____ plays on the slide.

    The baby   The woman   The boy

      ○   ○   ○

3. _____ swings.

    The baby   The boy   The girl

      ○   ○   ○

4. _____ helps the girl swing.

    The woman   The man   The grandma

      ○   ○   ○

5. _____ takes a nap.

    The baby   The boy   The man

      ○   ○   ○

Answer Key pages 1-9

Name_____ Date_____
Sentence or Not?

Directions:
Look at the pairs of pictures.
Circle the picture that shows a complete thought.
Make an X over the picture that shows an incomplete thought.

1. The girl. | The girl bakes cookies.
2. The boy rides his bike. | The bike.
3. The man cuts grass. | The man.
4. The baby. | The baby takes a nap.
5. The girl throws the ball. | The ball.

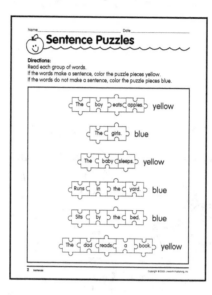

Name_____ Date_____
Sentence Puzzles

Directions:
Read each group of words.
If the words make a sentence, color the puzzle pieces yellow.
If the words do not make a sentence, color the puzzle pieces blue.

The boy eats apples. — yellow
The girls. — blue
The baby sleeps. — yellow
Runs in the yard. — blue
Sits by the bed. — blue
The dad reads a book. — yellow

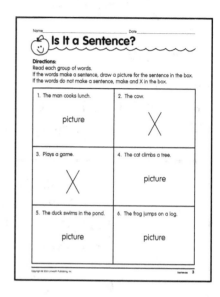

Name_____ Date_____
Is It a Sentence?

Directions:
Read each group of words.
If the words make a sentence, draw a picture for the sentence in the box.
If the words do not make a sentence, make and X in the box.

1. The man cooks lunch.	2. The cow.
picture	X
3. Plays a game.	4. The cat climbs a tree.
X	picture
5. The duck swims in the pond.	6. The frog jumps on a log.
picture	picture

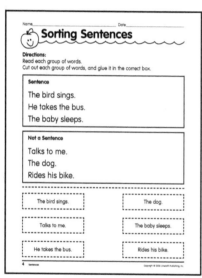

Name_____ Date_____
Sorting Sentences

Directions:
Read each group of words.
Cut out each group of words, and glue it in the correct box.

Sentence
The bird sings.
He takes the bus.
The baby sleeps.

Not a Sentence
Talks to me.
The dog.
Rides his bike.

The bird sings. | The dog.
Talks to me. | The baby sleeps.
He takes the bus. | Rides his bike.

Name_____ Date_____
Asking Sentences

Directions:
Read each group of words.
If the group of words is an asking sentence, color the bubble yellow.
If the group of words is not an asking sentence, color the bubble blue.

1. What are? — blue
2. What are you doing? — yellow
3. Can? — blue
4. Will she have a party? — yellow
5. Who is? — blue
6. Does she like cake? — yellow

Name_____ Date_____
More Asking Sentences

Directions:
Read the invitation below.
Then read each group of words.
If the group of words makes an asking sentence, answer the question.
If the group of words is not an asking sentence, circle the group of words.

Ryan will have a party!
You will spend the night at my house.
You need to bring a pillow.
We will eat pizza!
We will play games!
We will stay up all night!
Please come to my party!

1. Who will have a party? — Ryan
2. Where will? (circled)
3. What does? (circled)
4. What will they play? — games
5. What will they eat? — pizza

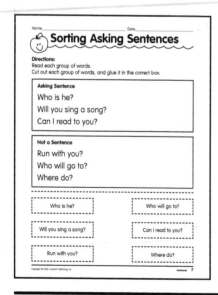

Name_____ Date_____
Sorting Asking Sentences

Directions:
Read each group of words.
Cut out each group of words, and glue it in the correct box.

Asking Sentence
Who is he?
Will you sing a song?
Can I read to you?

Not a Sentence
Run with you?
Who will go to?
Where do?

Who is he? | Who will go to?
Will you sing a song? | Can I read to you?
Run with you? | Where do?

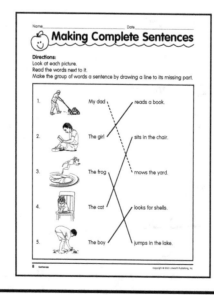

Name_____ Date_____
Making Complete Sentences

Directions:
Look at each picture.
Read the words next to it.
Make the group of words a sentence by drawing a line to its missing part.

1. My dad — reads a book.
2. The girl — sits in the chair.
3. The frog — mows the yard.
4. The cat — looks for shells.
5. The boy — jumps in the lake.

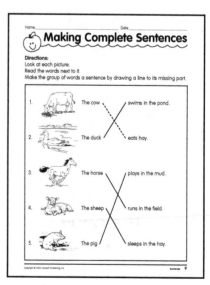

Name_____ Date_____
Making Complete Sentences

Directions:
Look at each picture.
Read the words next to it.
Make the group of words a sentence by drawing a line to its missing part.

1. The cow — swims in the pond.
2. The duck — eats hay.
3. The horse — plays in the mud.
4. The sheep — runs in the field.
5. The pig — sleeps in the hay.

Asking or Telling Sentences

Directions:
Read each group of words.
Cut out each group of words.
Glue it in the correct box to make a sentence.

Asking Sentence
Will you ride your bike?
Can you climb a tree?
Do you like to play soccer?

Telling Sentence
She plays soccer.
We ride bikes.
The boy likes to climb trees.

Will you ride your bike?	We ride bikes.
She plays soccer.	Do you like to play soccer?
Can you climb a tree?	The boy likes to climb trees.

10 Sentences

Ordering Words in Sentences

Directions:
Read each group of words.
Cut out each group of words, and glue them in the correct order.

1. Who is going to the party?

2. She talks on the phone.

3. We like to draw pictures.

4. What does he eat for lunch?

party?	to	going	Who	is	the
talks	She	on	phone.	the
pictures.	draw	We	to	like
eat	for	he	What	lunch?	does

Sentences 11

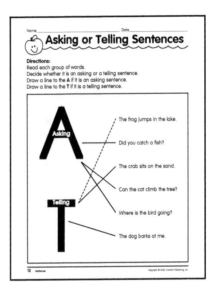

Asking or Telling Sentences

Directions:
Read each group of words.
Decide whether it is an asking or a telling sentence.
Draw a line to the **A** if it is an asking sentence.
Draw a line to the **T** if it is a telling sentence.

A Asking
T Telling

The frog jumps in the lake.
Did you catch a fish?
The crab sits on the sand.
Can the cat climb the tree?
Where is the bird going?
The dog barks at me.

12 Sentences

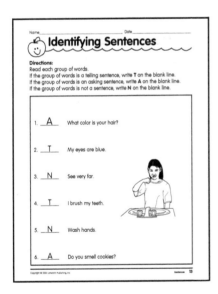

Identifying Sentences

Directions:
Read each group of words.
If the group of words is a telling sentence, write **T** on the blank line.
If the group of words is an asking sentence, write **A** on the blank line.
If the group of words is not a sentence, write **N** on the blank line.

1. **A** What color is your hair?

2. **T** My eyes are blue.

3. **N** See very far.

4. **T** I brush my teeth.

5. **N** Wash hands.

6. **A** Do you smell cookies?

Sentences 13

Writing Sentences

Directions:
Read each group of words.
Use the words to make an asking and a telling sentence.
Write the sentences on the lines.

1. help will you me
Asking: Will you help me?
Telling: You will help me.

2. will to me you read
Asking: Will you read to me?
Telling: You will read to me.

3. cake do like you
Asking: Do you like cake?
Telling: You do like cake.

4. a can ride bike you
Asking: Can you ride a bike?
Telling: You can ride a bike.

5. you my are friend
Asking: Are you my friend?
Telling: You are my friend.

14 Sentences

Reflect and Review

Directions:
Read each group of words.
If the group of words is not a sentence, circle the words.
If the group of words is an asking sentence, underline the sentence.
If the group of words is a telling sentence, underline the sentence two times.

1. The girl finds a shell.

2. Will you swim in the ocean?

3. The boys.

4. I like to go to the beach.

5. In the sand.

Sentences 15

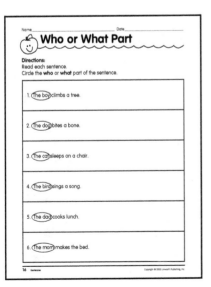

Who or What Part

Directions:
Read each sentence.
Circle the **who** or **what** part of the sentence.

1. The boy climbs a tree.

2. The dog bites a bone.

3. The cat sleeps on a chair.

4. The bird sings a song.

5. The dad cooks lunch.

6. The mom makes the bed.

16 Sentences

Does What Part

Directions:
Read each sentence.
Circle the **does what** part of the sentence.

1. The frog hops on a lily pad.

2. The fish swims in the lake.

3. The bear catches a fish.

4. The bird sits on a branch.

5. The goat eats grass.

6. The sheep drinks water.

Sentences 17

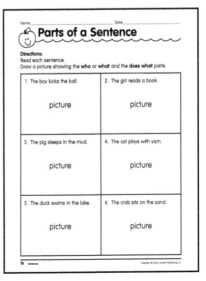

Parts of a Sentence

Directions:
Read each sentence.
Draw a picture showing the **who** or **what** and the **does what** parts.

1. The boy kicks the ball.	2. The girl reads a book.
picture	picture
3. The pig sleeps in the mud.	4. The cat plays with yarn.
picture	picture
5. The duck swims in the lake.	6. The crab sits on the sand.
picture	picture

18 Sentences

Answer Key pages 19-27

Identifying Parts of a Sentence

Directions:
Read each sentence.
Circle the **who** or **what** part.
Underline the **does what** part.

1. (The man) drives his car.
2. (The girl) kicks the ball.
3. (The boy) swings the bat.
4. (The mom) sings a song.
5. (The dad) reads a book.
6. (The dog) barks at the cat.

19

Identifying Parts of a Sentence

Directions:
Look at each picture.
Read the sentence beside it.
Answer the questions.

1. The girl opens the gift.
   Who or what? _____the girl_____
   Does what? _____opens the gift_____

2. The frog eats a fly.
   Who or what? _____the frog_____
   Does what? _____eats a fly_____

3. The sun shines.
   Who or what? _____the sun_____
   Does what? _____shines_____

4. The cat sleeps on my lap.
   Who or what? _____the cat_____
   Does what? _____sleeps on my lap_____

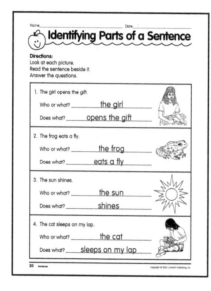

20

Making Complete Sentences

Directions:
Look at each picture.
Read the words next to it.
Make the group of words a sentence by drawing a line to its missing part.

1. The ant — barks at me.
2. The boy — rides his bike.
3. The girl — plays her game.
4. The dog — runs fast.
5. The lion — crawls on the log.

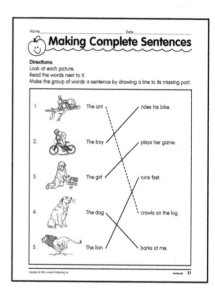

21

Writing Complete Sentences

Directions:
Look at the picture.
Read each **who** or **what** part beside it.
Choose the correct **does what** part from the choices below.
Write the word on the line.

Does What?

bite   talks   smells   sees   hear

1. The eye _____sees_____
2. The nose _____smells_____
3. The ears _____hear_____
4. The mouth _____talks_____
5. The teeth _____bite_____

22

Sentence Puzzles

Directions:
Read each puzzle piece.
Cut them out, and find the parts that go together.
Glue the parts together on a new page to make five sentences.

The girl	plays with a doll.
The dog	barks.
The bird	sings a song.
The fish	swims in the water.
The bear	climbs a tree.

23

Making Complete Sentences

Directions:
Read each group of words.
Draw a line from the **who** or **what** part to the correct **does what** part.

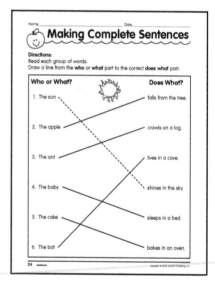

Who or What?	Does What?
1. The sun	falls from the tree.
2. The apple	crawls on a log.
3. The ant	lives in a cave.
4. The baby	shines in the sky.
5. The cake	sleeps in a bed.
6. The bat	bakes in an oven.

24

Finding the Who or What Part

Directions:
Look at the picture.
Read each **does what** part.
Choose the correct **who** or **what** part from the choices below.
Write the words on the lines.

Who or What?

The bird   The girl   The boy   The cat   The dog

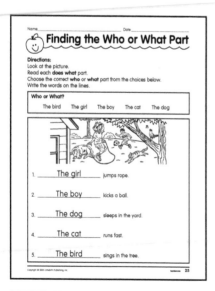

1. _____The girl_____ jumps rope.
2. _____The boy_____ kicks a ball.
3. _____The dog_____ sleeps in the yard.
4. _____The cat_____ runs fast.
5. _____The bird_____ sings in the tree.

25

Who or What & Does What Parts

Directions:
Read each sentence.
Write each part of the sentence in the correct box.

1. The dog runs.
2. The fish swims.
3. The bird sings a song.
4. The frog hops.
5. The horse eats hay.

Who or What?	Does What?
1. _____The dog_____	1. _____runs_____
2. _____The fish_____	2. _____swims_____
3. _____The bird_____	3. _____sings a song_____
4. _____The frog_____	4. _____hops_____
5. _____The horse_____	5. _____eats hay_____

26

Who or What & Does What Parts

Directions:
Read each sentence.
Color the **who** or **what** parts red.
Color the **does what** parts yellow.

red	yellow
The	duck	looks	for	food.
The	cat	climbs	the	tree.
The	fox	hides	by	a	rock.
The	fish	swims	in	the	pond.
The	goat	eats	grass.

27

Ordering Words in Sentences

Directions:
Read each group of words.
Cut out the words, and glue each one in the correct order.

1. The boy plays ball.

2. The girl jumps rope.

3. The baby sleeps.

4. The dog barks.

boy	plays	The	ball.
The	rope.	jumps.	girl
sleeps.	The		baby
barks.	The		dog

28 Sentences

Finding Parts of a Sentence

Directions:
Read each sentence.
Underline the **who** or **what** part.
Circle the **does what** part.

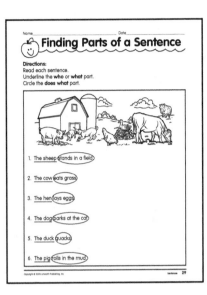

1. The sheep (stands in a field.)

2. The cow (eats grass.)

3. The hen (lays eggs.)

4. The dog (barks at the cat.)

5. The duck (quacks.)

6. The pig (rolls in the mud.)

Sentences 29

Reflect and Review

Directions:
Read each group of words.
If the group of words is not a sentence, color it yellow.
If the group of words is a sentence, color the **who** or **what** parts blue and the **does what** parts red.

blue The	**boy**	**red** eats	**lunch.**
blue The	**girl**	**red** sings	**songs.**
yellow The	**big**	**cat.**	
blue The	**man**	**red** reads	a	**book.**
yellow The	**baby.**		
blue The	**dog**	**red** barks.	

30 Sentences

Assessment 1

Directions:
Read each group of words.
Fill in the circle in front of the complete sentence.

1. ○ Goes to the store.
   ○ My friend.
   ◉ My friend goes to the store.

2. ◉ She rides a bike.
   ○ Rides a blue bike.
   ○ She.

3. ○ The school.
   ◉ We ride to school on a bus.
   ○ Drives a bus.

4. ◉ The man walks the dog.
   ○ The dog.
   ○ Walks the dog.

5. ○ The apple.
   ○ Falling from trees.
   ◉ The apple falls from the tree.

Sentences 31

Assessment 2

Directions:
Read each group of words.
Fill in the circle in front of the group of words that is not a complete sentence.

1. ○ My friend plays at my house.
   ○ We play games.
   ◉ Eat all the food.

2. ○ We run a race.
   ◉ Runs faster.
   ○ She wins the race.

3. ◉ Going to fish.
   ○ We go fishing in the lake.
   ○ We like to fish.

4. ◉ Hits the ball.
   ○ He hit the ball.
   ○ The boy swings the bat.

5. ◉ Draws a picture.
   ○ The girl can draw.
   ○ I like to draw.

32 Sentences

Assessment 3

Directions:
Read each group of words.
Fill in the circle in front of the asking sentence.

1. ○ Will?
   ◉ Will you help me?
   ○ Run for help?

2. ◉ May I have one cookie?
   ○ Bake some?
   ○ What can?

3. ○ What are?
   ○ Going to eat?
   ◉ What are you going to eat?

4. ○ To the store?
   ◉ Will you ride your bike?
   ○ Riding your bike?

5. ◉ Who is at the door?
   ○ The door?
   ○ Who is at?

Sentences 33

Assessment 4

Directions:
Read each group of words.
Fill in the circle in front of the telling sentence.

1. ○ Can you climb that tree?
   ◉ I like to climb trees.

2. ◉ The dog runs in the yard.
   ○ Do you see the dog?

3. ○ Where does the cat sleep?
   ◉ The cat sleeps on my bed.

4. ◉ I like red apples.
   ○ Do you like apples?

5. ◉ My friend jumps rope.
   ○ Can you jump rope?

6. ○ What is your favorite color?
   ◉ I like the color blue.

34 Sentences

Assessment 5

Directions:
Look at each picture.
Read the words next to it.
Fill in the circle in front of the words that complete the sentence.

1. The girl _____
   ○ sits in a chair.
   ○ rides a bike.
   ◉ jumps rope.

2. The frog _____
   ○ eats flies.
   ◉ hops on a lily pad.
   ○ swims in the pond.

3. The cat _____
   ○ takes a nap.
   ◉ drinks milk.
   ○ chases a mouse.

4. The bird _____
   ◉ sings a song.
   ○ flies in the sky.
   ○ eats a worm.

5. The pig _____
   ○ runs in the field.
   ○ eats hay.
   ◉ plays in the mud.

Sentences 35

Assessment 6

Directions:
Read each sentence.
Fill in the circle under the **who** or **what** part.

1. The fish <u>swims in the lake.</u>
   ◉   ○

2. My friend <u>plays baseball.</u>
   ◉   ○

3. My dad <u>drives a red car.</u>
   ◉   ○

4. The boy <u>reads a book.</u>
   ◉   ○

5. My grandpa <u>rides a bus.</u>
   ◉   ○

6. Her mom <u>likes to watch the game.</u>
   ◉   ○

36 Sentences

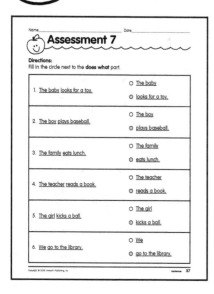

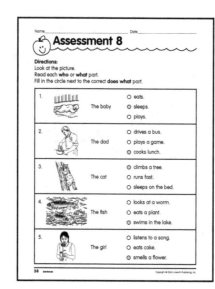

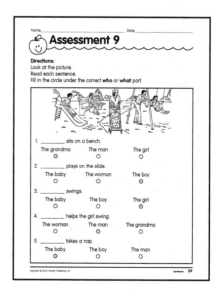

Assessment 7

Name_____ Date_____

Directions:
Fill in the circle next to the **does what** part.

1. The baby <u>looks for a toy.</u>
   - ○ The baby
   - ● <u>looks for a toy.</u>

2. The boy <u>plays baseball.</u>
   - ○ The boy
   - ● <u>plays baseball.</u>

3. The family <u>eats lunch.</u>
   - ○ The family
   - ● <u>eats lunch.</u>

4. The teacher <u>reads a book.</u>
   - ○ The teacher
   - ● <u>reads a book.</u>

5. The girl <u>kicks a ball.</u>
   - ○ The girl
   - ● <u>kicks a ball.</u>

6. We <u>go to the library.</u>
   - ○ We
   - ● <u>go to the library.</u>

37

Assessment 8

Name_____ Date_____

Directions:
Look at the picture.
Read each **who** or **what** part.
Fill in the circle next to the correct **does what** part.

1. The baby
   - ○ eats.
   - ● sleeps.
   - ○ plays.

2. The dad
   - ○ drives a bus.
   - ○ plays a game.
   - ● cooks lunch.

3. The cat
   - ● climbs a tree.
   - ○ runs fast.
   - ○ sleeps on the bed.

4. The fish
   - ○ looks at a worm.
   - ○ eats a plant.
   - ● swims in the lake.

5. The girl
   - ○ listens to a song.
   - ○ eats cake.
   - ● smells a flower.

38

Assessment 9

Name_____ Date_____

Directions:
Look at the picture.
Read each sentence.
Fill in the circle under the correct **who** or **what** part.

1. _____ sits on a bench.
   - The grandma ○
   - The man ●
   - The girl ○

2. _____ plays on the slide.
   - The baby ○
   - The woman ○
   - The boy ●

3. _____ swings.
   - The baby ○
   - The boy ○
   - The girl ●

4. _____ helps the girl swing.
   - The woman ○
   - The man ●
   - The grandma ○

5. _____ takes a nap.
   - The baby ●
   - The boy ○
   - The man ○

39

Printed in the USA
CPSIA information can be obtained
at www.ICGtesting.com
LVHW080724170724
785510LV00007B/294